Your Happy House

Illustrated Vāstu Shastra for Everyone

OLGA SOKOLOVA
(Mandodari)

Your Happy House

Illustrated Vāstu Shastra for Everyone

Mandodari International LLC

Frontispiece: Statue of Brahmarishi Mayan carved by masons in Mamallapuram's stone yard of Dr. V. Ganapati Sthapati, photographed by Olga Sokolova (Mandodari)

The information contained within this book is strictly for educational purposes. If you wish to apply ideas contained in this book, you are taking full responsibility for your actions.

Editor: Hank Goldstein
Illustrations: Alsu Halilova
Cover: Brenda House

First edition is published in the United States of America in April of 2017 by Mandodari International LLC, 530 S. George St., Charles Town, WV 25414
email address: om@mandodari.com
website: www. mandodari.com

Ordering Information:
Quantity sales. Special discounts are available on quantity purchases by corporations, associations, and others. For details, contact the publisher at the address above.

Printed in China

ISBN
978-0-9987405-0-8

Library of Congress Catalogue
Control Number: 2017904379

Dedication

To the ancient architect, the one of those who brought this knowledge on the planet Earth, to Brahmarishi Mayan of South India and to my guru, Padma Bhushan, late Dr. V. Ganapati Sthapati.

Olga Sokolova (Mandodari)
Charles Town, West Virginia
March 2017

CONTENTS

About the book

This book introduces ancient teachings about holistic design and construction according to Vaastu Shastra as it was revived and taught by south Indian traditional architect late Dr. V. Ganapati Sthapati from Chennai, India.

Your Happy House: Illustrated Vāstu Shastra for Everyone is mostly for the beginners in Vaastu (Vāstu) Shastra, and for homeowners, renters, architects, builders, and designers.

The idea was to create concentrated and easy to digest information, as well as to highlight the most significant and useful material for readers. This book includes:

- Basic theory of Vaastu Shastra
- Key requirements for designing new homes
- Practical tips on how to enhance your house
- Tips for buying a happy, peaceful and serene home

We hope that you will keep this small book in your pocket and the tips of ancient wisdom will help you to live your life in your home more happily.

Vaastu Shastra to Make You and Your House Happy

"To live in harmony with subtle nature is the aim of Vaastu science and technology."

- Dr. V. Ganapati Sthapati

This book introduces a modern, condensed view of the teachings of Vaastu Shastra, the ancient Indian theory of traditional architecture and design for temples and residential buildings. The history of Vaastu Shastra is several thousand years old. These Vaastu Shastra Wisdom pages are based on the teachings of a Tamil, South Indian traditional architect, Padma Bhushan Dr. V. Ganapati Sthapati.

Vaastu Shastra is the science of the space and time grid structure, spatial proportions, and divisions of the universal space. An architectural structure, fit properly into the inner grid of space, will achieve harmony and peace.

Personal Story

I arrived in Chennai at the beginning of January 2005, several days after the tsunami. I was not sure if I would be accepted to the educational course planned by Dr. V. Ganapati Sthapati six months prior to the horrific tsunami. Nevertheless, I arrived. It was my first, but not the last, visit to my future Indian Guru of Vaastu Architecture.

I left my shoes at the door and took several steps on the cool white marble floor. My heart pounded as I went upstairs to meet the world-renowned master. Dr. Sthapati (literally means architect) asked if I knew that the course had been cancelled due to the tsunami. I told him that I knew. I did not explain my stressful circumstances – I had gone through so much to be able to come: I had quit my job, purchased a non-refundable airline ticket and received all the required vaccinations. He asked me questions to determine what I knew about Vaastu, and concluded that I knew nothing. I agreed with his evaluation. Then he said, because I did not lie to him about my lack of knowledge, he will teach me. I could not believe my luck. I was ready to dance and hug my teacher!

12

Happy and Peaceful House

When all life energies are balanced with each other, there is Peace and Happiness.

Buildings are living organisms with their own energies. Humans have their own inner vibrations. Vaastu Shastra teaches how to balance life energies so they resonate like musical notes in harmony with our inner being, personality. If we follow Vaastu Shastra, we can create happy, peaceful houses and happy, peaceful people. Our house is an extension of our own character.

My Experience

During my course in India, I visited several Vaastu-built homes. I felt a gentle energy in these spaces. I felt peaceful. But at that time, I could not explain why. Later, I learned that Vaastu Shastra design involves very strict rules to balance the dwelling with the natural environment, use of natural materials, and to harmonize inner space with the inhabitants. Years later, after studying Advaita Vedanta and grasping the deeper knowledge, it became my life's goal to design "Happy Healing Houses."

Brahmarishi Mayan – Ancient Architect

The ancient architect Brahmarishi Mayan introduced Vaastu Shastra to humanity. According to old Dravidian texts, Mayan lived in Mahendra Parvata in Jamboodweepa, a sunken continent. His name is mentioned in several Indian scriptures as a great builder and technical wizard. Mayan authored and was written about in: *Surya Siddhantha* – ancient Indian astronomy; *Mayamatam* – treatise on architecture; *Aintiram* – Dravidian cosmology; *The Yogashastra*; Indian epics of Ramayana, Mahabharata; the Tamil epic of Silappathikaram, Manimrkalai, Jeevaka Chintamani.

My name Mandodari and Mayan

Dr. Sthapati could not remember my Russian name, Olga. He would refer to me as "madam." I asked my Teacher to give me an Indian name. After a short pause, he said, "Your name will be Mandodari," because even the tsunami did not prevent me from coming to study – I have something special in me. I must be connected to the ancient architect, Brahmarishi Mayan who had a daughter named Mandodari. I happily accepted my new, spiritual name.

Mandodari was married to Asura Ravana who became very learned after receiving Mayan's books as Mandodari's dowry. Brahmarishi Mayan was an extremely talented being who built many structures for kings and gods. He was not wealthy with worldly possessions, but rich with knowledge. So he passed his knowledge on to Ravana.

The literal meaning of Mandodari is "flat stomach." When my teacher's wife served me too much food, I joked that I will become "Gundodari" – heavy woman. This made my guru laugh.

A little statue of Mayan that I brought from India sits on my desk at home. When I do Vaastu design I ask my "father" to help me to design truly happy houses for my clients. It works!

16

Ancient Indian Palm Leaf Scriptures on Architecture

In India there are many ancient architectural treatises written in different scripts such as Grantha, Nagari and Sanskrit language. Ancient Indian scriptures were written on dried palm leaves inscribed with metal kernels. Then, the palm leaves were smudged with charcoal and cleaned, and the writing became visible.

Palm Leaves are Beautiful

Dr. V. Ganapati Sthapati inherited several suitcases from his father, also a temple architect and sculptor, containing ancient palm leaf scriptures. Dr. Sthapati told me his mother would get upset when his father purchased books instead of bringing home food.

These palm leaves were written mostly in ancient "technical Tamil." Dr. Sthapati was one of only a few people who could read and understand the language of his ancestors.

The palm leaves smelled of ancient times. I would become quiet and carefully hold the leaves in my hands. Then I would gently hug them close, imagining that the meaning from the leaves would fly into my heart to help me feel the knowledge.

Happy House, Happy Family

The goal of Vaastu Shastra is to create a happy home where humans will reach happiness, prosperity, serenity and spiritual bliss.

Each human has a unique inner sound. Every house has its inner sound. Every plant, every rock has its sound, etc. All forms of nature vibrate with life energy. The entire universe is singing. All sounds come from one primordial sound, "Om". The idea behind Vaastu Shastra is to orchestrate a beautiful symphony of sounds resonating in harmony to create feelings of happiness and balance between the owner and his house.

Feeling Peace and Happiness

I walked into a small tea house near Arches National Park in Utah, and I immediately felt peaceful there. Years back, I would have had no clue why I felt that way. Vaastu teaches the spiritual tuning of people to their houses and to Nature. Now I know that we feel peace where the interconnections inside a building are tuned. That tea house was tuned to the land and to the people.

The building's space is ringing and singing, and each person has an inner sound. Vaastu Shastra strives to bring feelings of peace and happiness by tuning subtle sounds of the building with the inner sounds of humans.

Vaastu Shastra gives detailed explanations and rules to find healthy land with good procreative energy; and how to connect the house with the land and with the people: how to pick a correct construction site; how to design beaming with the energy floor plan; how to find the right energy spot for a water pond; where to plant trees and shrubs to maintain good energy around the house; and even how to calculate the personal energy of each family member. The rules are not difficult.

21

Big Bang – Beginning of the Universe, of Time and Space

Once upon a time, there was no Time and no Space. There was one glowing Dot of Life Energy, Parabrahma, and around it a Great Void called "Sunyambaram" – the great potential and the great emptiness of everything. The experience of life entered and 'disturbed' the Dot. A huge strike of light flashed from the Dot, and an enormous explosion happened – The Big Bang. Light and sound filled the Great Void with particles of energy called "Paramanu". The emitted energy of light and sound is consciousness itself. The energy of consciousness completely fills the space of our universe.

Sitting at the pond and re-reading again and again

I'll never forget … sitting by a pond in a park near Gaithersburg, Maryland reading a magazine-size booklet titled, *Vaastu Purusha Mandala*, by Dr. V. Ganapati Sthapati.

The concepts describing time, space, light, sound and vibration of space were very different from anything I had learned studying architecture. Here, everything was alive and full of emotion – even houses were emotional entities. I had to repeatedly re-read to grasp such an unusual point of view. However foreign it was to me, I felt an incredible truth in these teachings. I decided at the pond that I would go to India to study the Big Bang of consciousness!

Paramanu – "Super Atom" – The Consciousness

In a state of peace – stillness – Paramanu has the shape of a cube, invisible to the human eye. The Great Void continued to fill with the light energy blocks, consciousness. In simple words, our universe is filled with Paramanus, the energy of life, and all material in the universe resides in this substratum. This is the energy substance of the Space. In the center of the Paramanu there is a small dot called "Brahma Bindu" – the center of concentrated consciousness. The creation of everything begins in Brahma Bindu.

The size of the particle of Paramanu was described in Surya Siddhanta, an ancient astronomy text authored by Mayan, and Manasara, an ancient architectural treatise.

I could not imagine that consciousness has shape!

Consciousness has shape in space and can be measured. It took me years to accept this concept.

Imagine a very small particle of energy inside of you, in the area of your physical heart, glowing with golden light. It is your personal consciousness, connected through space with the universal consciousness. We are "swimming" in the ocean of consciousness.

Universal consciousness pulsates and creates forms – these forms are thoughts and dreams. When we think, we concentrate our thoughts, creating a small dot of energy in our own small particle of consciousness! From that concentrated dot of consciousness dreams emerge.

Dance of Consciousness

When Thought comes into the Universe, a string of Light – the movement of consciousness – appears in the Brahma Bindu, the center of Paramanu. What scientists call the "Super String Theory," Hindu philosophy calls "the Dance of Siva Nataraja", the Great Dance of Space. The Supreme String 'dances' and causes the Paramanu cube to spin. In Vaastu Shastra this 'super string' is called "Brahma Sutra", the line of light and creation. As a result of the spinning, Paramanu becomes spherical. The sphere is energy manifested into material form. Thus, all *material* particles in our universe are spherical: our body parts, molecules, atoms, planets, suns, etc.

My head is spinning
Think, think and think

When you become tired from thinking, you may say, "My head is spinning from my thoughts." According to the teachings, you really spin inside when you think – your particle of energy spins during your thought process. Tiny strings of light appear inside of your particle of consciousness. You emit waves of energy, waves of your thoughts.

You use huge amounts of your energy when you think. You can become exhausted from the spin of your own consciousness. Your string dances and dances until you stop thinking – if you can. Meditation and yoga are techniques that can help stop your inner spin, your uncontrollable flow of thoughts.

Siva Nataraja – Great Dancer of the Universe

Siva Nataraja performs the Panchakritya Thandava Dance, creating the universe, emitting energy. He stands on the dwarf, or demon, Apasmara (Muyalaka in Tamil). The image of Siva standing on the dwarf symbolizes victory over the ego, or ignorance.

You are small Siva Nataraja

Dancing Siva Nataraja has a string of light going through his body, a bright beam of pure consciousness. He creates the universe by emitting energy – particles of Himself – into the void. He spins the energy to make it beam with light and sound.

Siva created the universe including you and your little particle of conscious energy, which increases or decreases based on the pattern of your thinking. Like a small Siva Nataraja, you also beam with light energy when you think and dream.

28

Dimension of Paramanu – Measurement of Consciousness

Paramanu is the smallest unit of space measurement, the Primal Energy Unit. When Thought comes into the Universe, Paramanu begins spinning, gradually changing into a sphere called "Anu". In *Indian Sculpture and Iconography,* Dr. Sthapati defines the Anu as, "... one part of $190,650^{th}$ of an English inch and hence not perceptible to the naked eye."

The middle state of the transformation of Paramanu – from cube to sphere – is octagonal. Teachings say that Paramanu as a cube represents a peaceful state of energy, pure consciousness, also called the "Sattvic state". The Paramanu in an octagonal shape in 3D is the middle state of consciousness or "Rajasic state" – movement, agitation. The last stage of consciousness transforming into matter is when Paramanu becomes a sphere which is "Tamasic state" of consciousness, the state of inertia.

Can form influence our consciousness?

When studying architecture at the Architectural University of Saint Petersburg, Russia, I learned about different architectural styles, shapes and colors, but nothing about how buildings can influence our consciousness. We all see and feel architectural exterior-interior beauty or ugliness. Why do we feel differently about the buildings?

Vaastu Shastra teaches the importance of dimensions and forms of a building. The dimensions can be discordant or harmonic based on the unit of measurement and building's proportions. The shape of the building sets the quality of the energy in the building, directly influencing our life and ability to work.

Square and rectangular-shaped buildings have peaceful energy – they serve well as residential, educational and general work environments. Round buildings spin the energy inside. Hence, people who live in round buildings will tire faster and will not feel peace. But they are good for entertainment. An octagonal-shaped building is between stillness and spinning. It is recommended for market places.

The source information about sacred geometry comes from the Fifth Veda, which includes Vaastu Shastra, the origin of sacred geometry.

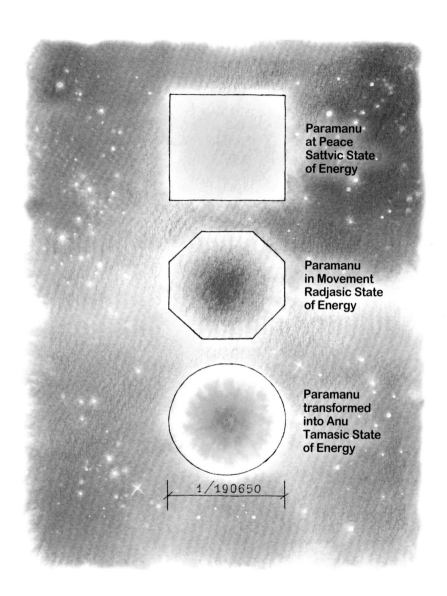

Paramanu
at Peace
Sattvic State
of Energy

Paramanu
in Movement
Radjasic State
of Energy

Paramanu
transformed
into Anu
Tamasic State
of Energy

1/190650

Ancient Architectural Scale – Measurement of Consciousness

A Paramanu multiplied many times to the tangible dimension for construction, is called an *"angula"* or *"viral"*: a finger-breadth, about 1 3/8 of an inch. The ancient scale is called "Kishku Hasta", or Cubit. It is made up of 24 angulas. A Kishku Hasta may vary in length from 31-33 inches.

According to Vaastu Shastra, dimensioning in inches is acceptable because inches correspond to the human body – a living organism. Measuring with centimeters will not work.

Buildings measured by this scale are alive because they fit into the structure of the space.

Trying to get in the airplane with Kishku Hasta

While studying in India, I asked my teacher if was possible to purchase a Kishku Hasta, the ancient architectural scale. Instead, Dr. Sthapati gave it to me as a graduation gift.

The graduation was very special. I received a diploma and a calendar with photographs of our classes. The wooden Cubit was brought to me from the Puja room, where my Teacher's wife blessed it with red kumkum powder and yellow turmeric powder. Then Dr. Sthapati said, "Put this stick on your altar and worship it! This is a very important instrument."

The course was over and I had to go home. My priceless Kishku Hasta (33" long) didn't fit in my suitcase. I held it in my hands as a carry-on item. I was stopped at customs because my wooden stick was too long. I explained that it was a gift from my Guru and begged to let me carry it on. I could not leave India without my 'scale of the Universe', a gift from the Guru. To my happiness, the Indian officials let me on! Kishku Hasta sits on my altar.

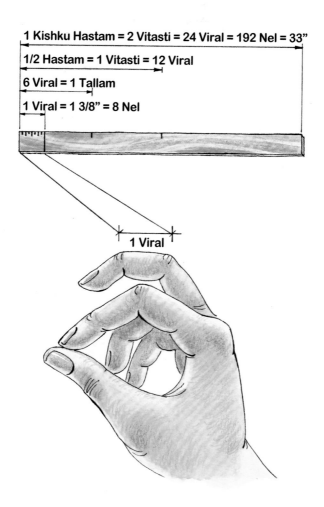

1 Kishku Hastam = 2 Vitasti = 24 Viral = 192 Nel = 33"

1/2 Hastam = 1 Vitasti = 12 Viral

6 Viral = 1 Tallam

1 Viral = 1 3/8" = 8 Nel

1 Viral

Absolute Time is Vibration of Space

All of space is filled with energy. This energy vibrates in pulses of eight, considered a most sacred number. Space expands in sequences of eight. Vibration in eight is the pulse of the universe. One set of eight pulses at the source is equivalent in duration to a blink of an eye. It is the unit of the Absolute Time, the rhythmic breath of the universe.

One blinking of an eye – eight pulses of the universe

Number eight is the most sacred number in Vaastu Shastra.
Imagine a source of universal energy that gives birth to waves of light energy, filling the void with particles of light; a roaring sound following waves of light emerging from the source. The explosions in the energy center occur in sequences of eight. This process is called, "Absolute vibration of the universe." The period of time for the universe to send eight pulses is equal to one blink of a human eye.

We, humans, blink in unison with the universe. We are linked with our bodily functions to the periodic, rhythmic pulses of the universe.

34

Adi Tala – Inner Sounds in people and buildings

Vaastu Shastra teaches that Absolute Vibration of space - the primordial pulse of the universe, or burst of energy - comprises eight beats (musical notes). After a set of pulses, space pauses and sends another sequence of eight beats. The time cycle of eight beats in traditional Indian Carnatic music is called "Adi Tala". In Sanskrit Adi Tala means primary rhythm, or primary clap. In Vaastu Shastra it is Absolute Vibration. Universal Space sings and expands with each set of pulses. In this way, Time and Space are interconnected.

In traditional architecture and sculpture, the expansion of space is incorporated into a special scale. The unit of the scale derives from the dimension of the human palm. In Carnatic music, each beat has its own sound akshara - musical note. There are eight notes in total: Sa, Ri, Ga, Ma, Pa, Dha, Ni, Sa. The human body can be divided vertically into a grid of eight full Tala - palms lengths - plus one more Tala derived from the lengths of joints (1/4 Tala) of the body which makes the total height of the body equal to nine Talas. Each complete Tala has a corresponding musical note. So, we have all the musical notes in our body singing.

Buildings have proportions in Talas, and the height of a building should also be nine Talas. The goal of Vaastu Shastra is people in harmony with buildings and the universe by harmonizing the inner subtle sounds of the building with the inner subtle sounds of people.

Are you nine palms tall?

My teacher once told me, "please measure your right palm and then multiply by 9. See what dimension you get." My palm measured 19.3 cm or (7 5/8 inches). Multiplying by nine arrived at 173.7 centimeters or (5' – 8 5/8"). Wow! Almost exact! I thought, Vaastu Shastra works! Try it for yourself and see how nine units of your palm matches your body height or your energy grid.

This means that all musical notes Sa, Ri, Ga, Ma, Pa, Dha, Ni, Sa are singing, and the parts of the joints add their sounds to make a unique sound inside of us.

Vaastu Shastra calculates this to match a building and a person to sound harmonically together and coexist in peace.

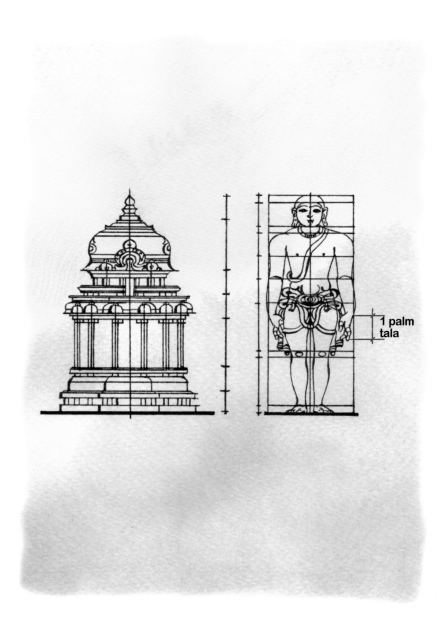

1 palm
tala

Manduka Mandala – Grid of Absolute Love

Space is packed with Paramanu. Paramanu explodes into multiple copies of itself. The emitted energy is Om light and Om sound. Energy organizes itself into the grid, creating the structure of the universe. The 8x8 grid, the Manduka (frog) Mandala, is the matrix of the universe.

According to Vaastu Shastra, the universe is built from grids of 8x8 in two dimensions, and 8x8x8 in three dimensions. All space is a grid of Absolute Love – everything is made of Absolute Love.

Buildings for worship and residential buildings

Vaastu Shastra prescribes designing buildings using specific grid systems to establish inner qualities of a building's space. An even grid brings peaceful, serene, blissful Divine energy; an odd grid, materialized energy. A floor plan of a building using an even numbered grid (4x4, 8x8, 16x16), is suitable for worshipping. A floor plan using an odd grid (9x9, 11x11, 13x13), is suitable for residential or commercial use.

Absolute Vibration of the Universe in eights

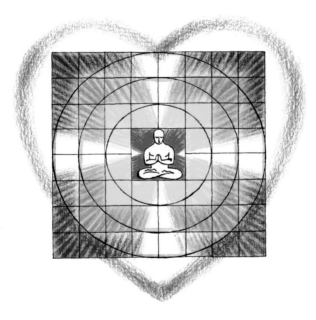

Manduka Mandala

Universal Grid of Energy

"It is this love that holds everything together. And it is everything, too."

-Rumi

When we build according to Vaastu Shastra, we build happy homes because they fit proportionally into the grid of Absolute Love.

Absolute Space made of Absolute Love

I continued my education to better understand Vaastu Shastra. I started learning yoga and Advaita Vedanta (non-duality). I learned that beyond forms, beyond time and space, is only essence, "Sat Chit Ananada", which means, "Existence Knowledge and Bliss Absolute." In simple terms – unconditional love.

By the force of unconditional love, space was created. Space contains the universal grid of energy. If architects follow the rules, fitting houses into a grid structure, into the streams of peaceful energy, then they will help us to experience more peace in our homes.

Grids in the Brain

An article titled "Secrets of the Brain", published in the February 2014 issue of *National Geographic* magazine, describes neuroscientist Van Weeden's discovery of a grid structure in the brain. Our brains pass information through neurons; and, according to Van Weeden's research, they intersect at 90-degree angles.

It makes sense: the universe passes information produced by consciousness in the grid system called "Vaastu Purusha Mandala". All human beings and animals have neurological grids. Vaastu Purusha Mandala is a 'highway', or flowing energy of thought.

Modern science is catching up with ancient knowledge!

Is our science getting closer to the ancient wisdom?

The author of the National Geographic article, Carl Zimmer, tells us a story about Van Wedeen's discovery: "As he increases the magnification, something astonishing takes shape. In spite of the dizzying complexity of the circuits, they all intersect at right angles like the lines on the sheet of graph paper ... Wedeen is more convinced than ever that the pattern is meaningful. Wherever he looks – in the brains of humans, monkeys, rats – he finds the grid." I emailed the neuroscientist and he replied, "This grid is like a scaffold, like 3D graph paper."

Dr. V. Ganapati Sthapati taught about 3D grid of the universal space in 2005 in Chennai. It would be fantastic to compare the dimensions of the brain grids with the Paramanu dimension. We should find the spatial connection between distances of the intersecting neurons and the invisible structure of space, mentioned in the Shastras.

We Create Grids Too

Human beings create space. We expand the universe when we think. A mini Big Bang happens inside of us when we generate a new thought.

The same small particles of energy reside inside of us. It is our true self, the true thinker and creator in us. In Hinduism this particle of consciousness is called "Jeevatma". When we think, we emit energy. This energy goes into space and adds more energy to the universe. Dreaming creates the energetic structure of a thought, like a hologram. Our thoughts reside in the space attached to us like a 'balloon', or energy structure, and then manifest.

Can't you feel from far way that your boss is angry?

Imagine yourself sitting in your cubical at work. All you see is your computer screen and your desk. Then 'something' comes and you feel uncomfortable, something is wrong. You suddenly think about your boss who was not happy about you or your work. Then you learn that your colleague saw the boss walk near your workspace as the 'dark cloud' appeared. You may say to yourself, "it is my great intuition!" You are correct, but also it can be explained as energy moving though the space.

We emit energy when we think. The energy can be 'heavy' if our thinking is negative. This 'negative wave' moves through the space and enters your cubical. You feel it right away because you are also energy.

It is not a bad idea to consult with a Vaastu practitioner to help you identify problems in your workspace and suggest how to improve it. You can check, for example, if your boss sits under a ceiling beam – which can make a person moody. Beams 'cut' spatial energy and negatively influence the person whose desk is beneath the beam.

44

Manifesting your Perfect Home!

By dreaming about our perfect home and visualizing the details, we actually create a holographic image of the house in a layer of subtle energy, which can manifest materially. If we doubt our dream, we "remove" particles of energy from the picture – like removing pieces from a puzzle. When we continue to visualize our perfect home, the image strengthens – and it will manifest. You can do it!

Personal dream materialized

At the end 1980's, Russia was going through tremendous changes. I was dreaming of coming to the United States to live, but it seemed totally impossible to me and my friends.

I listened to songs about America. I found a small American flag patch and asked my mother to sew it onto my shirt pocket. I wore it to work. I asked my close girlfriend, Lidia if she would go to America with me. She told me that I, "looked into the dark sky from the window of my apartment and I was somewhere far away", when I said that. I was DREAMING big time! I was creating holograms of my future life.

I have now lived in the United States for many years. My friend Lidia still asks me how it was all possible. Many people were dreaming to go to the America but from our circle of friends, only I went.

Keep dreaming and dreams will really come true!

46

Resonating grids of energy

In order to build a happy house, we need to harmonize energies. The cosmic energy, Earth energy, human energy and the house's energy should resonate. The grid of the cosmos, the grid of the planet and the human grids should be aligned. Earth naturally fits the cosmic grid. All we need to do to achieve harmonic resonance of grids and a happy house is to align the house with the parallels and meridians of the planet, the energy lines of the Earth.

Are you looking for a new home?

Rule number one in Vaastu Shastra is to check the position of the house on the planet Earth. If the building is shifted about 45 degrees from the direction of meridians or parallels, it is totally off from the energy grid of the planet. There is even a name for that in Vaastu Shastra: "Vidik," meaning the energy in this house is weak and "against" the stream of energy of the planet. It's better not to move into such a house.

48

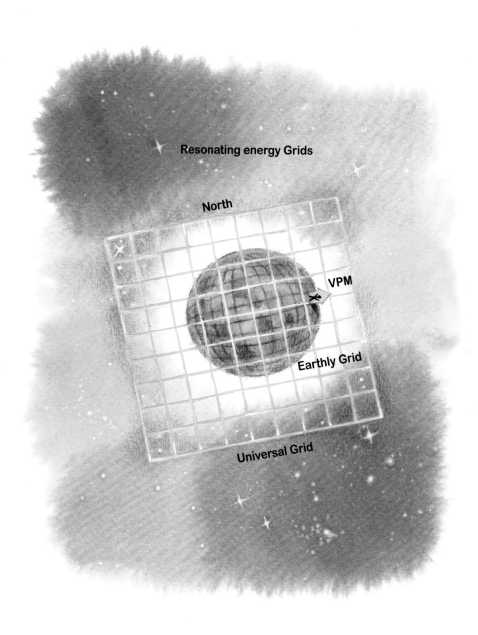

Vaastu Purusha Mandala

Life energy permeates all space in the universe, and organizes itself into grids. A mandala is energy organized in a grid pattern. The lines of the grid are conduits that channel the energy.

Initially, energy organizes itself into the Manduka Mandala: an 8x8x8 grid. It then transforms into a 9x9x9 grid, a Paramasayka Mandala. "Pranava", the transformation from eight to nine is like the embryo in an egg becoming a chick.

The 9x9 grid in two dimensions serves as the baseline for a blueprint of a house. The entire grid is filled with the life energy, called "Purusha". Each cell in the grid represents a specific energy or deity. Energy of different qualities, both positive and negative, are balanced in the body of the grid.

Do you have a name to your house? Give it a good happy name!

Everybody likes personal attention. So does Purusha, the energy that lives in your house. Give him a nickname, a real name that resonates with you. Purusha will "like" it. A good and happy name for the house will help to transform the energy of the house for the better.

My husband and I own an old historic property. Our house looks like a small castle. My husband named our house, "Maison Du Soleil" – house of the Sun. We both like it, and Purusha likes it too.

Become a friend with your house, with the energy of the house. Sing songs in the house. He will "sing" with you. Clean your house, decorate with love and attention, and make it cozy.

Paramasayka Mandala 9 x 9

Chladni Patterns and Vaastu Purusha Mandala

Ernst Chladni, an 18th century German physicist and musician, demonstrated that different frequencies of sound create consistent patterns of standing waves. Are these patterns the same as Vaastu Purusha Mandalas?

In 2003, Steven Lehar, a researcher from Boston University wrote in his paper *Harmonic Resonance Theory*, "Harmonic resonance of a different form has already been identified in biological systems in the field of embryological morphogenesis, where the principle of reaction diffusion has been identified as the system that defines the spatial structure of the developing embryo by way of chemical standing wave patterns."

According to the teachings, Vaastu Pursuha Mandalas are subtle structures of harmonic vibrations of Light and Sound. These vibrations create specific designs, like Chladni patterns, and are used to create harmonics in the basic design of the Vaastu house.

Resonate with your house and with Nature

Your inner energy (soul) sings inside of you with a subtle, specific sound. This sound can be heard during deep meditation. The sound creates a mandala, a design like Chladni Patterns. Your inner sound pattern is unique. You are a unique geometric structure.

If you are stressed or upset, your inner sound becomes disturbed; your mandala becomes a little faded.

A Vaastu house designed and built for you and your family will be constantly charging you, keeping your energy vibrant and intact. It will keep your energy in harmonic resonance not only with the house, but also with Nature.

Your house is connected with the planet and with the cosmic energies. You, your house, planet Earth and cosmic energy are resonating harmonically.

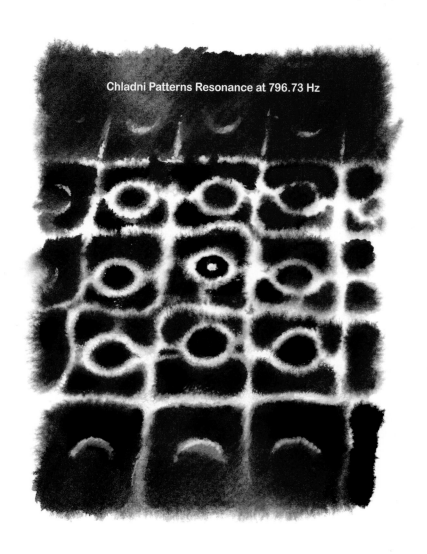

Chladni Patterns Resonance at 796.73 Hz

Pancha Mahabhutas – Five Great Creative Elements of Nature

Creative forces mix energy in a specific ratio – the Panchikaranam Process. Pancha Mahabhutas, the five creative elements, enter into existence and settle in the Vaastu Purusha Mandala.

Each corner, and the center of the grid, corresponds to a Creative Element. The central part of the grid - Space (Akasha), the northwest corner - Air (Vayu), the southeast corner - Fire (Agni), the northeast - Water (Jala), and the southwest corner - Earth (Prithvi). Each element has a unique inner property, or frequency of vibration. Vaastu Purusha Mandala, the matrix grid for the floor plan of the building, is aligned with the direction of true north.

Every corner of your house has its own quality

Vaastu Shastra has a recipe for the floor plan of a building – the Vaastu Purusha Mandala. Just as we have a skeleton, so the building should have a proper skeleton of energy and energy "organs" to maintain its healthy life.

Energy distributes itself in the 'cells' of the building. The center of the building has very light, lively and sparkling energy. Every corner of the building has its own vibrancy – cool, hot, watery, heavy – and its own purpose according to these qualities. Just as the cells in our bodies do what they need to do, the same goes for our houses.

Knowing all this, we can develop floor plans using the natural qualities of the space in the building to achieve harmony: cooking space where energy is hot; sleeping space where energy puts you to sleep; and so on.

True North

NW   NE

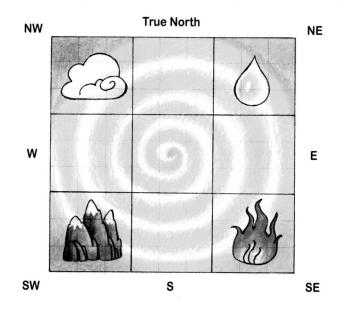

W   E

SW   S   SE

Five Creative Elements and Healing Balance

Humans are also composed of Pancha Mahabhutas, the five universal creative elements. They dominate in different parts of our body. When the elements move from their proper locations, our bodies can become sick.

A floor plan designed according to the principles of Vaastu Shastra allows the house to use energy of the grid properly, based on the inner qualities of the space. For example, we would place the kitchen at southeast corner where the space has the quality of fire. To promote deeper sleep, we would place the bedroom at southwest corner where the quality of the space is earth. In doing so, we can create natural, invigorating, healing environments.

Connection between Ayurveda and Vaastu Shastra

Ancient Ayurveda is preventive naturopathic medicine from India. It heals with herbs, massage therapy, diet and lifestyle changes to bring life into balance.

Like Vaastu Shastra, Ayurveda works with energy fields. Ayurveda considers the body and organs as a continuation of the person's energy field. Personal energy fields have the same types of energies as the house: Space, Air, Fire, Water and Earth. Vaastu Shastra balances life energies in the house, and Ayurveda balances the body.

Ayurvedic scriptures even contain information about Vaastu Shastra. For example, if person has too much Fire energy, Ayurveda recommends sleeping in the northeast corner of the house, the Water zone, until the person heals. If someone feels fatigue, she can spend time in the Fire zone to energize herself. Each situation is unique and treated individually during Ayurvedic and Vaastu Shastra consultations.

The illustration shows distribution of major types of energy (doshas) in the human body. Easy moving Space and Air energies help a person to move around. Fire energy helps digestion. Earth and Water energy keep us grounded.

Earth
Water

Fire

Air
Space

57

Locations of Rooms in the House

The Vaastu Purusha Mandala, the energy grid, has five creative elements distributed in a special order over the grid. We use the inner qualities of the space in the house according to its subtle qualities.

The central part of the house, Brahmasthan, should be empty and can be used for special occasions.

- The northeast corner of a building (Water) – good for a meditation room, or home office;
- The southeast corner (Fire) - the kitchen;
- The southern zone - dining rooms;
- The southwest corner (Earth) - the master bedroom;
- The western zone - the family room;
- The northwest corner (Air) - good for children's or elders' bedroom;
- The northern zone - Living Room (reception room).

If your rooms are not in the right place

I teach internationally through Sivananda Vedanata Yoga Centers in Europe and the Americas, and in my home country, Russia. My students often ask, "What we do when the rooms in the existing home are totally in the wrong locations and not according to the rules of Vaastu Shastra and the Vaastu Purusha Mandala."

Some people use remedies – symbols, pyramids, etc. – attempting to fix a problem with the space. However, Dr. Sthapati taught that only structural changes or physical changes can fix a problem.

There can be a "rectification" of the house. For example, sleeping in the Fire zone makes people irritable. Can you move your master bedroom from Fire zone (SE) into the Earth zone (SW)? Look carefully at the floor plan and try to change all possible functions of your rooms based on the Vaastu Purusha Mandala – the inner energy of the space. Do what you can to improve your situation. It will help.

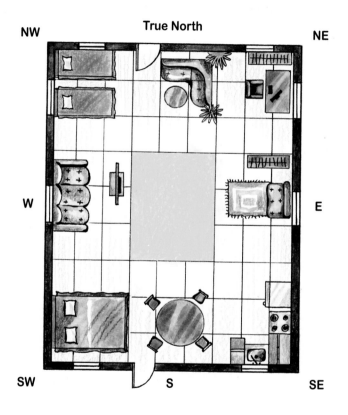

W   E

Brahmasthan - Nuclear Energy Field in the House

A house receives subtle energy from the Cosmos and the Earth, and from material energy such as solar radiation, energy from the underground water, as well as from soil, trees, etc. The environment influences not only the material building, but also the subtle energies contained within.

Space has a grid system (mandala). The central part of the grid, Brahmasthan – the nuclear energy field – is the most concentrated and powerful. It is the 'lungs' of the house.

The central part of the house, or the 3x3 part of the 9x9 grid, must remain empty. There should be no structures like toilets, laundry rooms, elevators, pillars, interior walls, etc. to 'clog the lungs' of the building. Brahmasthan, the middle part of the house, the place of Creation, allows energy to spread in the entire house.

Do you feel depressed in your home or claustrophobic?

I'm not a doctor, but this is what I've learned: if you feel down in spirits, like something is suppressing you at home, then check the Brahmasthan area of your house and in each of the rooms.

Why must the central part of your home be EMPTY? The central part of the house has very lively energy, called Akasha in Sanskrit. Akasha has the potential energy to help you manifest your dreams, to remove obstacles in your life, and to keep your family together in a friendly atmosphere. It is the nuclear energy of your house. To work for you, it has to be free from obstructions.

Each room has its own mini Brahmasthan. Remove clutter from the center of each room in your house. Move away heavy furniture. Let your house breath happily. You will feel the difference.

A man came from Germany to Canada where Dr. Sthapati was lecturing in 2007. He brought a, to scale, model of his yoga home where he lived with his wife and son and taught yoga classes. My teacher immediately told him, "Sir, as soon as you can, remove this structural column from the center of the Brahmasthan. Otherwise, you will divorce your wife!" Years later, this man reported to Dr. Sthapati that he saved money to make structural changes to the space, and it made many aspects of his life easier.

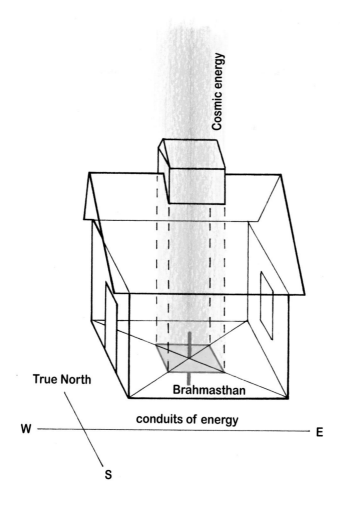

Cosmic energy

True North

Brahmasthan

W ——————————— E

conduits of energy

S

Ayadi Calculations – Tuning Your House to the Universe and to You

Vaastu contains a precise mathematical tuning called "Ayadi" calculations. The primal energy particle is also called "Adi". "Ayadi" means to analyze primal energy. The Ancient architect would do Ayadi to achieve a resonance of energies between the cosmos, Earth, the house and the family.

Everything vibrates and creates musical sounds. The Universe has its own primordial sound, "Om." Each human has his or her own inner sound. The house, too, vibrates with sound. Ayadi calculations prescribe precise perimeters and height for house to create a natural symphony between living energies.

When we are in tune with our house, we exist in harmonic resonance with nature and the entire Universe, we are healthier.

If your house is not calculated per Ayadi but the rest is good

When we asked our teacher this question, he said that in older times it was not difficult to build with correctly calculated dimensions. Nowadays, with prefabricated materials, it is difficult and expensive.

However, a healthy house can be designed and built according to the rules and principles of Vaastu Shastra, even where Ayadi calculations are not possible.

What is the difference then? An Ayadi calculated house is like a tailor-made dress, specifically for you. A non-Ayadi house – a dress purchased from a department store – can be very beautiful too.

If you sell your house, calculated for you and for your family, the next family will still benefit from a Vaastu House, tuned to nature in many different ways.

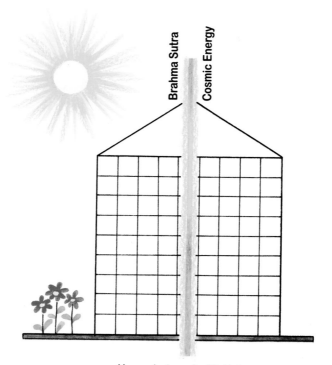

House in-tuned with Nature

Selection of the Building Site for Healthy House

In ancient times, cows and bulls would be brought to test a potential building site. If they ran happily and tried to mate, this demonstrated that the land had a good vibration. Nowadays, we can bring house pets. If they are happy and playful, then it is good place to build.

A level slope is best. Soil color should be even: white, red, yellow, black and grey soils bring wealth and prosperity. The texture should be soft, close-grained, well-consolidated – but not clay-like. When tapped, the soil should sound like a horse or an elephant (it has very deep sound when tapped); it should taste sweet, bitter, astringent, saline and sour. These qualities bring wealth and prosperity. Trees with thick green leaves and land overgrown with fragrant flowers are good signs.

Avoid swampy soil, marshlands, brownfields, old graveyards, broken stones, tiles, scraps of iron, rats, white ants, snakes and frogs. These indicate cancerous land.

Feel the energy of the land where you want to build

When you are looking for land to build on, pay attention to the environment: are the people around happy and welcoming? Is the vegetation healthy and green; are flowers growing and birds singing? These are signs of good energy. Always trust your first emotions about the area, before the mind starts calculating.

Real estate agents say, "location, location, location." Yes, it is important what the location is. Does the energy of the region fit your inner energy? If you need activity, look for places where things are happening. If you are looking for seclusion and quiet, look to be near parks, trees, etc. Simply look at your inner qualities and find something to balance you and make you happy. Trust your intuition because, according to Vedanata philosophy, it is your higher mind.

Proportions of Residential Buildings

A building requires specific proportions. We capture energy in the volume of the building. The proportions create specific energetic vibrations in the house. There are five basic proportions for floor plans for positive harmonic vibrations:

1 : 1   1 : 1.25   1 : 1.5   1 : 1.75   1 : 2

Proportions and beauty

Do you sometimes feel lost or squeezed in a building? It may mean that the building's proportions are off.

Vaastu Shastra design follows very specific proportions – nothing is random. Sizes of buildings are determined in relation to an Ayadi calculated modular system. Just as our bodies have a specific, optimum proportion, the same is true for buildings.

Vaastu Shastra says that the last touch of the Creator in the stages of creation is decorating a "bold" form. (Maybe that is why we like to decorate our houses, ourselves – we are conducting the last acts of the creation.) Beauty can be seen and felt in the harmony of forms, colors, architectural embellishments, interior decorating, etc. Beauty is in balance.

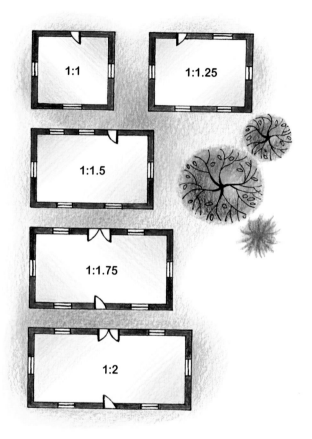

Best Level of Underground Water for a Healthy House

Water naturally emanates strong subtle life energy, and absorbs additional energy. To avoid disturbing the balanced energy of the building, underground water should not be higher than the height of an average man with raised hands – about seven and one-half feet or deeper – from the base of the foundation of the building.

Did Frank Lloyd Wright make a mistake in his Fallingwater house design?

The Fallingwater house in Pennsylvania, designed by Frank Lloyd Wright, is considered a masterpiece of modern architecture – impressive and well-merged with the environment. However . . .

According to Vaastu Shastra, living above water is not recommended. There is constant movement of energy in moving water. If a house sits over a waterfall, the energy is overbearing for humans. This moving energy penetrates the entire house, including the people, leaving no peace.

Peace is in silence and stillness of the thoughts. To reach peace we need to reach inner silence. Serenity in nature is very helpful. It is good to have a creek near the house but not under the house.

From the perspective of Vaastu Shastra, Frank Lloyd Wright made a mistake positioning the house on the waterfall. I wonder if the family of Edgar J.Kaufmann, Fallingwater's owner, felt relaxed in the building.

7' - 6"

Underground Water

Clock-wise direction

Best Positions of Doors and Windows

The Vaastu house is based on the 9x9 energy mandala, or Paramasyaka Mandala. Each cell (pada) of the mandala has either positive or negative energy. Overall the entire mandala is balanced energy wise. Good house design positions the main door in the proper pada. The pink color squares in the figure indicate good positions for doors, in order to have a positive effect. Good door locations in the Northern hemisphere (counting clockwise from left to right):

From **North** – 3, 4, 5 are good padas.
From **East** – 3, 4 are good padas.
From **South** – 4, 6 are good padas.
From **West** – 3, 4 padas are good.

Using any other locations–padas–for a main entrance will have a negative effect. Ayadi calculations will produce the exact direction for the main door to yield the maximum benefit.

In the Southern hemisphere the mandala should be mirrored along its Southern side, which parallels the equator.

Did you know that your front door could bring you success in life?

Definitely, a beautifully designed front door makes your house more attractive and makes you feel proud about your house.

The location of the front door charges energy entering your house. If your door is in the pada of the Vaastu Purusha Mandala – which gives you riches – you will be successful in business. If your front door is sitting in the pada of fear, you will be affected by fearful thoughts. Every cell, or spatial module, of your house is charged with a specific quality of energy. If your door is in a positive energy cell, you will be lucky; if not, you are out of luck.

True North

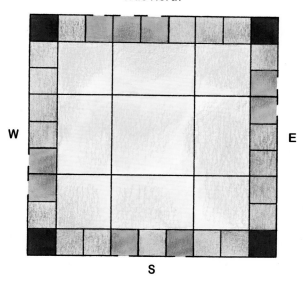

W

E

S

Good Entrances in Pink
Pramasayka Mandala 9x9

Best location for Bathrooms and Staircases

In ancient times, outhouses and bathhouses stood separate from the main building. Today, the best location for bathrooms is in the additions, outside of the main grid of the house. Bathrooms can be placed inside in the main grid at northern or eastern zones, but not directly in the northeast or southwest corners: these corners are considered sacred. The same rule applies to the septic tank. Water wells should be placed in the northeast zone outside of the house because it is the property of Subtle Water. Staircases should direct the movement of people up to the next level in a clockwise direction. They should not be installed in the Brahmasthan area.

My old house and falling down from the staircase

Now, I understand why I didn't feel comfortable in our old house. Our house was built in 1940. It was nice looking from the outside – a two-story brick house with about 2000 S.F. of living area. We made some great interior decorations and improvements.

Our favorite room was a verandah with large glass windows and filled with plants. The space felt very cozy, and we spent most of our free time there. The room was totally open in the center and had so much light. But... As soon as you enter the front door, you almost stumble into the staircase. The staircase was built right in the center of the house, three feet off the main door, dominating the space. It splits the house into two separate areas, creating not only a feeling of a 'small house', but a feeling of suppression. One evening, I left our bedroom to go downstairs, wearing wool socks and no shoes. A thought flashed through my mind: "I don't want to fall down." As soon as I took a step, I fell to the bottom of the staircase. I made an incredible noise, counting every wooden step with my elbows, and landed on the last step. As I landed, the front door opened wide and someone came in. I didn't even have a chance to cry. The visitor asked me if I was OK. I was not OK. But I thought, "How inconvenient to have this staircase right next to the front door. I cannot even cry." Intuitively, while living in that house, we always wanted to move this staircase to the side of the house. Instead, we moved out. In our current house, the staircase in the perfect place – on the side – and it feels right. Now I know that the staircase in the old house obstructed the energy field, and we could not feel peaceful there.

72

True North

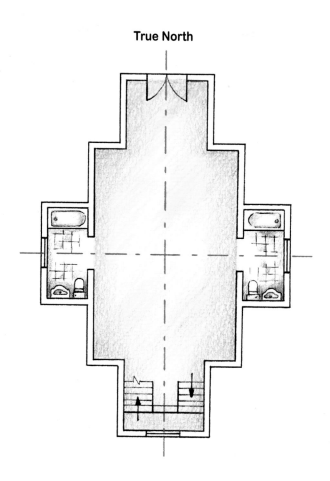

Sample Floor Plan of Vaastu Healing House

The drawing shows a floor plan for a simple Vaastu Shastra Happy Healing House: a small cabin, using the Paramasyaka mandala 9x9 grid. The cabin is oriented according to cardinal directions to align with the Earth's energy grid. The front door is in the positive pada in the South. The *Brahmasthan* is empty and clear to facilitate energy distribution.

Swami's Little Hut

Once, I was given a task to design small cabin for a monk. The place had to be small, and the entrance was restricted to the south. When I did Ayadi calculations for the Swami, I was surprised that the calculations matched the requirement-restriction to place the door in the south.

Ayadi calculations show not only the perimeter of the building but also some other information such as direction (Yoni) for the main door. Yoni means that specific direction will be the best for this person or persons.

There is also a meaning to each direction, e.g., south is for those who seek salvation and don't care about the financial gain. In this project, the Swami abandoned ideas about financial gains a long time ago: the southern entrance was good for the swami in many different ways.

True North

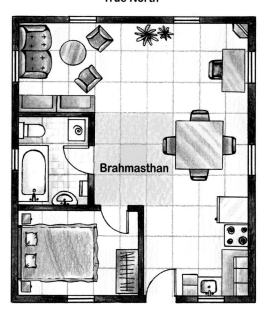

Brahmasthan

Roof Slopes for Residential Buildings

The roof can be viewed as a 'prism' through which Divine light will refract. Roof slopes are set to specific angles. By using these slopes in the figure, the architect creates a good energy vibration in the house. The ideal slopes proportions are as shown in the drawing: 3:4:5 (3 rise/4 run); 4:3:5 (4 rise/3 run); 5:12:13 (5 rise/12 run); 12:5:13 (12 rise/5 run).

Is roof of the house appearing as energy lens?

In *Sthapatya Veda* Dr. V. Ganapati Sthapati quoted Robert Lawlor's *Sacred Geometry* book many times, so I decided to read *Sacred Geometry*. I found an interesting discussion about angles on page eight:
"Likewise, geometric optics reveals that each substance characteristically refracts light at its own particular angle, and it is this angle which gives us our most precise definition of the substance. Furthermore, the angles in the bonding patterns of molecules determine to a great extent the qualities of the substance."
According to Vaastu Shastra, space is packed with Paramanu (Divine Energy). The energy inside any space is influenced by the shape. The roof can be viewed also as an 'energy prism', refracting Divine light coming from the cosmos. Setting the slope of the roof sets up specific energy fields in the building.

76

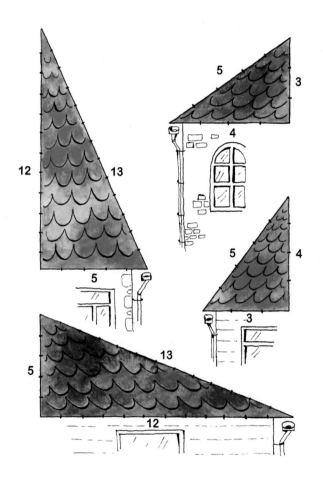

Cardinal Directions and their Qualities for the House

Cardinal directions – South, North, East, West – bring different qualities of Energy to the house. The front entrance functions like the 'mouth' of the building and 'inhales' energy. Each cardinal direction corresponds to a quality of Divine energy:

- Energy from the north is associated with Kubera, and brings wealth.
- Energy from the east is associated with Indra, and brings comfort.
- Energy from the south is associated with Yama, and brings salvation for the soul.
- Energy from the west is associated with Varuna, and brings prosperity.

According to the teachings, doors should not be located at the corners of the building.

Your Energy and Directional Energy

Imagine the universe expanding in all directions. The stars and constellations send us signals as electromagnetic radiation – and so much more we neither know nor see. The universe contains expanding and spinning directional energies – we are part of the energies.

A goal of Vaastu Shastra architecture is, with the help of the house, to align ourselves with the movements of universal energy.

In India, people do not like their houses facing south, knowing that the Southern God Yama is a God of death. Vaastu Shastra teaches that every direction can provide benefit, even facing south. Why is that? In order to align harmonically with the Universal energies, you need a portion of one type of energy, and somebody else needs a portion of another type of energy. Energetically, south may bring what this person needs.

Where should the front door of your house be placed to establish peace for your family? Using Ayadi calculations, we can determine the directions that suit you and your family members. We need to align your energy, the house's energy and the directional energies of the universe into one river of energy where you flow like a boat along the Divine River.

Brings Comfort In Life
East

Brings Material Wealth
North

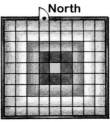

Brings Salvation
South

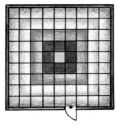

Brings Prosperity
West

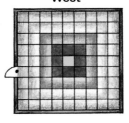

How to Find Cardinal Directions

A house should be almost aligned with the cardinal directions of the map. All maps show true north, not magnetic north. True north, geodetic north, points towards the geographic North Pole. Magnetic north moves and can only be found with a compass. Vaastu Shastra uses true north.
It is easy to find true north for a house with "Google Earth" or "Google Maps". Enter the physical address into the software and see how the house is positioned according to the cardinal directions. The house should be aligned as much as possible for better energy circulation and balance.

Looking at Portland, Oregon from the bird's eye view

My husband and I went to Portland, Oregon for business several years ago. On the second day, after we finished our work, we took a tramway to get a good feel for the city.

We both liked the streets: people sitting outside on the terraces laughing, many cozy restaurants. It really felt happy and inviting. We were travelling from east to west. When the tramway crossed the river, I immediately felt sadness: the streets were empty, here and there were homeless people.

I wondered what was missing. I checked the city map. Across the river, in the entire eastern side of the city, the streets are perfectly aligned with the energy grid of the planet. Back across the river in the western side of the city, the grid is turned 45 degrees (Vidik in Vaastu Shastra). Wow!

Because of a 45 degrees shift, the western part of the city is a big mixer of energy that never stops. The eastern side of Portland is more beneficial for business growth, for happy living. The energy of the planet charges people naturally and gives them peace if the built environment is in alignment with Vaastu Purusha Mandala. It would be very beneficial for city planners to follow the ancient rules of Vaastu Shastra and see the difference.

I would like to take on a project evaluating cities: comparing economic data, crime statistics, business growth, etc., and see how it follows the predictions of Vaastu Shastra.

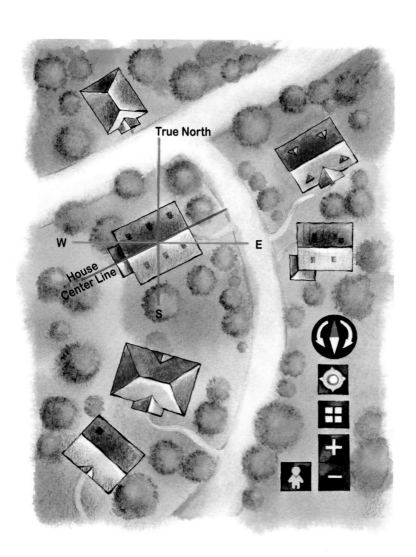

No Cutting Corners in the Building

The corners of the building are zones with concentrated energy. We cannot 'cut corners' of the building as a part of the architectural design. To do so risks losing a great amount of energy, leading to more stress. Similarly, to prevent the loss of energy, windows should not be installed in the corners of the building.

Why are the Icons for prayer in the corners of the room?

How interesting ... in the Orthodox tradition, icons for prayer are always placed in the corner of the room. I suspect the energy concentrated in the corners energizes the objects. Vaastu Shastra suggests having your icon or prayer at the Northeast corner of the room, or Northeast corner of the house, where the subtle Water energy has a soothing quality.

Cutting corners – loosing energy

Properly Positioning House on the Property

The architect has to position the building along the grid lines of the planet to properly align with the Universal energy. In most cases, property lines and street lines are not aligned with meridians and parallels – the energy grid of the planet – so houses should not be positioned along property lines or street lines. This drawing shows the correct positioning of the house on the property.

Looking for house to purchase and feeling the energy

My daughter, in the process of house-hunting, asked me to give her quick suggestions about the houses she was considering. When I explained some basic rules of Vaastu Shastra to her, she began to notice how houses feel based on their position and inner layout. She said houses that are aligned with cardinal directions rather than aligned to the street feel more peaceful. The peacefulness was especially present in houses with open floor plans where the Brahmasthan area was not blocked with structures or interior walls.

She said, "Vaastu works, I see it now!" I was happy to hear another endorsement of the ancient teachings through the personal experience of my daughter.

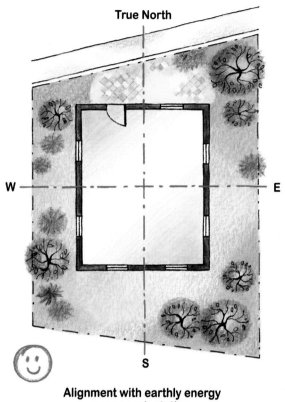

Alignment with earthly energy
proper orientation

Incorrect Positioning of House on the Property

The drawing shows the incorrect positioning of the house on a property which parallels the street line.

House is not flowing but fighting with the stream of energy

Where the street is not aligned with the cardinal directions, and the house is aligned with the street line, the house is like a boat moving against the current of the river, fighting with the stream of energy and losing its own energy. Depending on the person, an uneasy sensation arises slowly and cannot be recognized immediately. Very sensitive people feel the subtle stream of energy right away.

Knowing the rules of Vaastu Shastra, we can avoid mistakes and find a peaceful home.

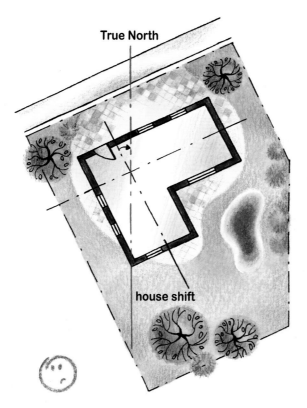

True North

house shift

Offset from the energy grid of the earth
Incorrect orientation

Good and Best Slopes for the House

Vaastu Shastra scriptures identify a variety of natural slopes of the Earth with detailed descriptions of the slopes and their meanings. Slopes indicate changes in the energy field of the planet. There is pressure from above, and there is a counter-pressure of energy from the planet's core. The surface of the planet presents a plane of stabilized energy.

Good slopes benefit the house and people; bad slopes take away energy. For example, land that slopes from east to west takes away material wealth. The best and simplest way to create a balanced energetic environment is to build on flat land.

Can slope "take" your money away?

Improper slope can take your money away! How is this possible?

Vaastu Sastra scriptures identify more than twenty slopes with specific qualities. For instance, a slight eastern slope is good for political leaders; a slight northern slope is good for intellectuals such as teachers, doctors, lawyers, scientists, etc. If north-west is higher on your property, it is easier to sustain financial losses. If north-east is higher, sadness comes. If west is higher, expect increase in family. If south is higher, freedom from diseases comes.

The best and the simplest situation is flat land: the energy of the flat land is balanced and most peaceful.

NE – East

Negative influence

SW – West

Balanced energy – positive influence

89

Street Lines and House

Moving objects in the street have their own energy, which contacts the structure, disturbing the energy balance of the house. Streets must not dead-end or intersect at the house. The centerline of a cul-de-sac crosses the house, disturbing the energy in the house. See the example drawing.

If house is "hit" by the energy of the street, what to do?

What can you do if your house is 'hit' by the disturbing energy of the street? The easiest protection from disturbing energy is trees and shrubs planted parallel to the house as a wall of living energy. Vaastu Shastra suggests planting along the energy of Vaastu Purusha Mandala of the house. Trees and shrubs 'hold' the energy around the house and protect against disturbances from the outside. Fences and stonewalls are also good. In older times, people would build dry-stack knee walls to hold energy around the entire property.

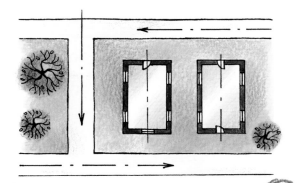

Street energy passes by – no influence on the house

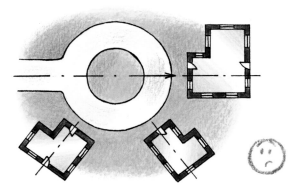

Street energy directly hits the house – negative influence

How to Fix Property Lines

The grid lines of the Universe intersect at ninety-degree angles. Irregular shapes – not ninety degrees – conflict with Universal motion and create unbalanced energy. Fences built along irregular property lines introduce instability in the energy field.

Fence lines should be corrected to ninety-degree intersections. Landscape architects should draw rectangular shapes of the maximum possible size within the existing property line to resolve the problem. Fences can be installed, or trees and bushes planted to create a balanced shape with right angles along these corrected lines. It is enough to plant a tree or bushes at the corners of the new rectangular shape to strengthen the energy field of the house.

After I fixed property lines, what do I do with the leftover land?

The illustration shows how the irregular shape of the property lines is 'fixed' with a fence or green border. The corners and parts of the property beyond corrected lines are good to use for gardening, garages, garden sheds and other secondary type structures.

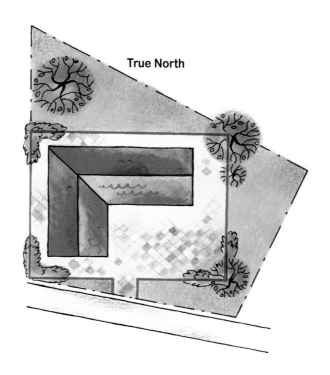

True North

Fixing irregular property lines along earth's energy field

Most Useful Suggestions for the Prayer Corner and Your Home Office

The "freshest" energy comes with the rising sun. When you sit at your desk, facing east will help you to think clearly. The northeast corner of a house or room is the Water Zone – the corner of peace and tranquility. You can establish an altar there with any divine images that are close to your heart – saints, prophets or even pictures of nature – which calm your mind and make you happy. You can hang a picture of a waterfall, sunrise, etc.

If my North East corner of the house is not available, where do I pray or meditate?

Your house has an inner energy structure – rooms have the same small Vaastu Purusha Mandala grids imbedded in each other. The grid exists on a smaller scale in each room. If it is not possible to situate your relaxation space close to the northeast corner of the building – the subtle Water zone or peace zone – use any other suitable room in your house. Find north east in that room, and place your altar there.

94

Desk facing East for clear mind

How to Get a Good Sleep

The Earth is aligned with the energy flow in the Universe. To sleep peacefully, humans need to align with the grid of the planet. Vaastu Shastra recommends sleeping along east-west lines of the Earth, with your head facing one of these directions. Another good position is to sleep with your head facing south. Avoid sleeping with your head toward north or along diagonal (NE, SE, SW and NW) directions.

Compass on smartphone helps to find correct direction to sleep

Energy moves from south to north. Vaastu Shastra says to avoid facing your bed toward the north where you would be in the constant current of energy, which does not allow for deep sleeping.

When I travel, I use a compass on my phone to find true north in the room where I will be sleeping. Once I locate north, if I can, I change my bed position, or at least arrange my pillow to the correct direction. At home, try moving your bed to sleep in the preferred direction. Then see if your sleep is deeper.

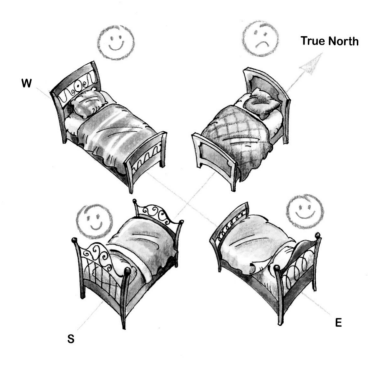

Positive and negative directions for sleep

Sleeping in the Attic

If your bedroom is in the attic, locate the bed under a flat part of the ceiling. If you sleep with your head under the sloped ceiling, energy slides along the ceiling line, preventing deep and peaceful sleep.

Feeling restless in the attic bedroom or under cathedral ceiling

Lecturing about Vaastu Shastra takes me to different countries, different cities and different rooms to sleep. Several years ago, while lecturing in Siberia, I stayed in the home of one of my students. I vividly remember the bedroom in the attic. My small bed was tucked under the steep slope of the ceiling. I could not sleep comfortably under the sloped attic ceiling, however I did not want to offend my student and ask for a different room. I tried to relax and not to think about the improper placement of my bed. I felt the pressure of the ceiling. My sleep was not deep.

Energy under an attic ceiling is not at peace because it is moving along the sloping ceiling lines. Furthermore, the space is 'cut', and therefore disturbed. Energy at peace has shape of the cube – Paramanu. 'Cut' Paramanu space forces the energy to move. One easy solution is to move your bed under the flat part of the ceiling. Another is to create a flat ceiling above your head with a canopy. You will feel cozy in your canopy bed and should sleep deeper.

Good sleep under flat ceiling only

Solve Most Common Problem – Remove Clutter

The most important part of the building is its central part, the Brahmasthan. And, each room has its own Brahmasthan. Removing clutter from the center of the room stabilizes energy and will bring you peace.

Create cleaner, energy-wise surfaces by removing unnecessary things. Less furniture allows energy to distribute freely about the house. Divine energy gets 'stuck' in the clutter of the attic – clean your attic. Cleaning stabilizes the energetic environment and brings you health and happiness. You feel better in a clean, uncluttered environment.

Trust your intuition when organizing your space.

Allow creative force to be free and happy

I returned from India with some very good books related to Vaastu Shastra, and a laminated diagram of Vaastu Purusha (the soul of the planet Earth). Vaastu Purusha is drawn inside the Vaastu Purusha Mandala. Purusha's head is in the northeast corner of the mandala and his belly is in the center. His navel is in the exact center of the mandala. There are different deities – forces of creation – shown in cardinal directions. Brahma with four heads sits in the center.

According to Hindu philosophy, Brahma is creative force, and it is in the center of any room and in the center of the house. By removing clutter from the center of the room or house, we allow creative energy to energize us, uplift us, help us with our own creativity and make us feel free and happy.

No mess in the center of the room – high energy area - Brahmasthan

Major requirements when looking for a new house

1. Minimum building's shift in the relation to the cardinal directions (true North, South, East , West) is no more than
   1-2 degrees off the true North toward NE when main door is facing North or South
   1-2 degrees off the East toward NE when main door facies East or West.
2. Main door should not be at the corner of the building if single family home.
3. The best shape of the floor plan of the house should be rectangular or square.
4. Central part of the building, the Brahmasthan should be empty (no bathrooms or staircases in the Brahmasthan).
5. No sleeping under the sloped ceilings.
6. Look for healthy vegetation on the property.
7. Slope on the property - flat land is the best.
8. Best if garage is attached to the main building.

Vaastu Barn-House in Poolesville, MD designed strictly per Vaastu Shastra by design group of Mandodari International LLC. Photograph by Hendrick J. Sterenberg

About Padma Bhushan Dr. V. Ganapati Sthapati

 Padma Bhushan Dr. V. Ganapati Sthapati (1927 – 2011) was a world renowned traditional architect, and specialist in the field of Vaastu Shastra. He belonged to the eleventh generation of traditional temple architects. Dr. V. Ganapati Sthapati was also a well-known teacher, lecturer and sculptor. He implemented the knowledge in Vaastu Shastra or Sthapatya Veda in many of his projects. Dr. Sthapati wrote more than 35 books about Vaastu Shastra, including *Building Architecture of Sthapatya Veda* and *Indian Sculpture and Iconography*. He established by his death will the Vaastu Vedic Trust in Mamallapuram, Tamil Nadu to continue his research and teachings. Vaastu Vedic Trust has a website: – **www.Vastuved.com**.

Photo above by Olga Sokolova (Mandodari), Dr. V. Ganapati Sthapati in his school of Vaastu Shastra. Mamallapuram (2009).

104

About Olga Sokolova aka Mandodari

Olga Sokolova (Mandodari) is a disciple of Dr. V. Ganapati Sthapati. She received her certification as Vaastu Shastra Consultant from the International Institute of Mayonic Science and Technology, Chennai, India in 2005 after completing classes conducted by Dr. Sthapati. Mandodari was born in Saint Petersburg, Russia and now resides in the Washington D.C. metro area, USA.

She received her Master's degree in Civil Engineering from Architectural University of St. Petersburg, Russia and Associate in Arts and Science degrees in Interior Design, Montgomery College, Rockville, USA.
She also received a Ph.D. from The Open International University for Complementary Medicines, Colombo, Sri Lanka, affiliated with The International Institute of Integral Human Sciences, Montreal, Canada. Mandodari also received Yoga Siromani Diploma from International Sivananda Yoga Vedanata Center in Grass Valley, California, USA.

According to the Death Will of Dr. V. Ganapati Sthapati, Mandodari is a Member of the Vaastu Vedic Trust, Mamallapuram, Tamil Nadu, India. She consults clients, continues her research and lectures internationally.
More information about Olga Sokolova (Mandodari) and her work can be found at her websites:
www.mandodari.com
www.meditationvimana.com.
Photo above: Olga at the stone yard of her Guru in Mamallapuram, India in 2009; photo on the left: Olga and her husband Hendrick Jan Sterenberg with Dr. V. Ganapati Sthapati at his house in Chennai, India in 2009.

Alsu Halilova, the artist illustrator

 Alsu Khalilova is an artist from Moscow, Russia. She has created illustrations for this book that speak for themselves. She graduated from the Moscow Art School in Memory of 1905. The artist is a member of the Moscow Union of Artists.

Alsu is a professional illustrator and illustrates books for children. Her work is mainly in watercolor. Personally she is a soft and intuitive soul but also a well-established perfectionist.

We worked together on the illustrations for almost a year. Alsu made many versions of each illustration. Sometimes I had to ask her to stop improving each illustration to perfection, as it already reached the point. She wanted to grow into this topic with all her mind and soul, and to do all that is possible to make it perfect. She certainly succeeded.

Many thanks for Alsu for her thorough and inspiring work! I hope readers will enjoy the illustrations.

Hank Goldstein, editor

 I've known Hank for several years. He is a great song writer, singer, guitar and drum player. He feels life in all its intricacies and aptly captures this in his songs. I am very grateful that he agreed to edit my book – otherwise my "Russian-English" would show up on every page.

Bibliography

Dr. V. Ganapati Sthapati, *Building Architecture of Sthapatya Veda*, 1st and 2nd ed., Chennai: Dakshinaa Publishing House, 2001 and 2005.

Dr. V. Ganapati Sthapati, *Ayadi Calculations*, 1st ed., Chennai: Dakshinaa Publishing House, 2003.

Editor and English translator P. K. Acharya, *Manasara Series*, Delhi: Low Price Publications, 2004.

Prof. S. K. Ramachandra Rao, *The Agama Encyclopedia*, 2nd ed., Delhi: Sri Satguru Publications, 2005.

Tarapada Bhattacharyya, *The Canons of Indian Art a Study of Vastuvidya*, 3rd ed., Calcutta: Firma KLM Private Limited, 1986.

English Translator and editor Dr. S. P. Sabharathnam, Tamil version compiler Dr. V. Ganapati Sthapati, *Mayan's Aintiram*,1st ed., Madras: Vaastu Purusha Publishing House, 1997.

Editor Bettina Baumer, *Kalatattvakosa*, Vol. One, Revised ed., New Delhi: Indira Gandhi National Center for The Arts, 2001.

English Translator and editors Alice Boner, Sadasiva Rath Sarma, Bettina Baumer, *Vaastusutra Upanishad*, 4th revised ed., Delhi: Motilal Banarsidass Publishers, 2000.

Olga Sokolova, *The Postulates of Brahmarishi Mayan*, 1st ed., Saint Petersburg, Russia: Mandodari International, LLC, 2009.

Your Notes: